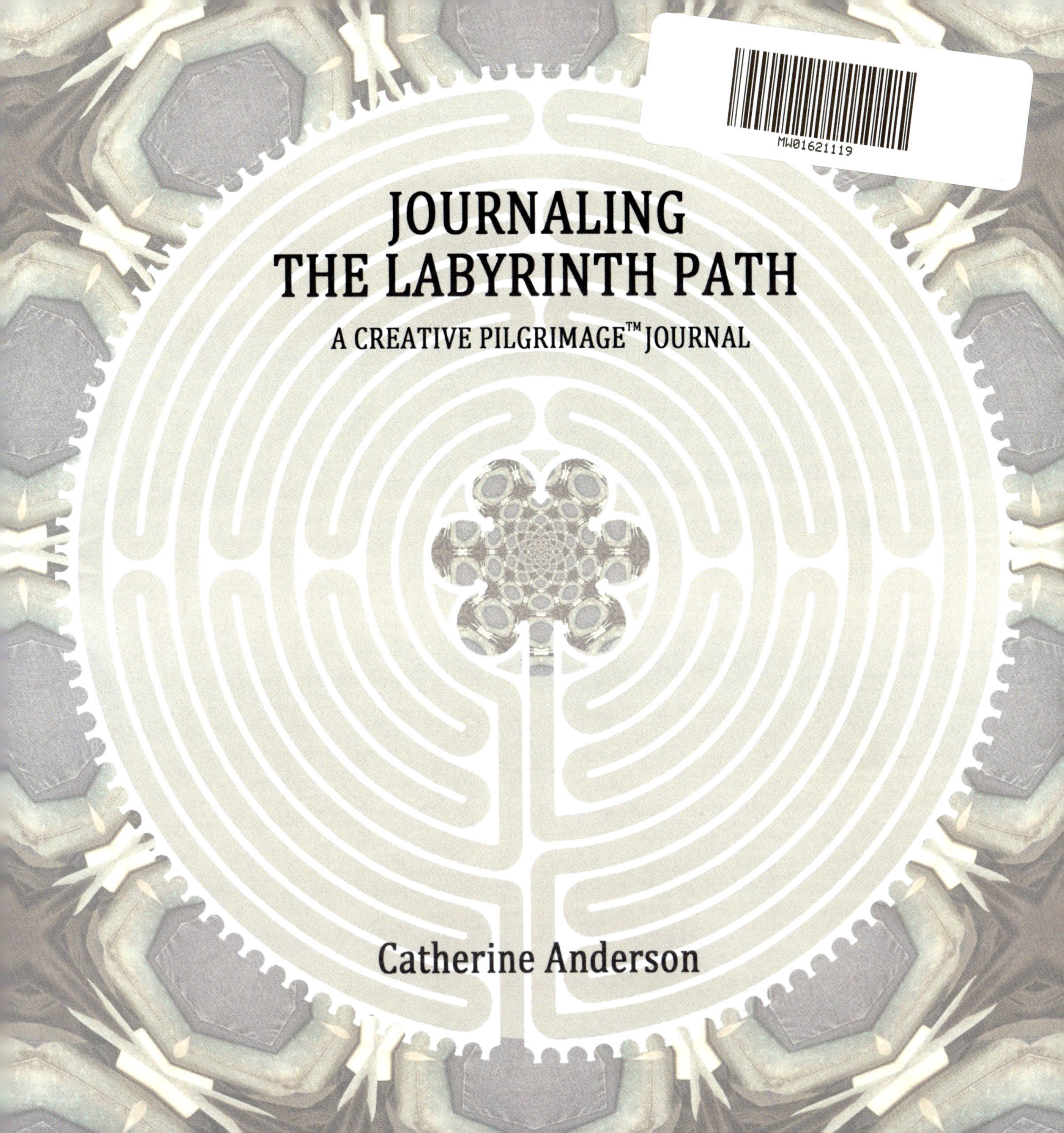

JOURNALING THE LABYRINTH PATH

A CREATIVE PILGRIMAGE™ JOURNAL

Catherine Anderson

www.CatherineAndersonStudio.com

ISBN-10:098852712X
ISBN-13:978-0-9885271-2-6

USING THIS JOURNAL

You can't always retreat from the world to a country house, the seashore or the mountains.
But it is always in your power to retreat into yourself.
Marcus Aurelius

We are not all fortunate enough to have a labyrinth in our backyard to walk whenever we feel the call to connect with the winding path of the labyrinth. This journal can be a place to turn when you yearn for the calming path of the labyrinth.

The labyrinth provides me with a quiet, still center, a place where I can listen deeply. It is a place to come back to myself when life has been frantic or stressful. The labyrinth can remind me of who I am and gently guide me back into balance.

I have created this journal to be used as a place where you can walk the labyrinth with your words and with your fingers as they touch the page with the writing of your pen. Let your words tumble out without judgment as you move around the path of the labyrinth. Turn the book as your write.

You can do this practice with just one word, with an affirmation, with a pattern, or you might choose to reflect on the quotation or journal prompt. However you feel called to play on the page is the right way. You might be influenced by the colors on the page or the image behind the labyrinth. Follow your intuition.

You can return to the same labyrinth again and again. You don't have to complete your journaling in one sitting. As you would when walking a labyrinth, be aware of anything that happens while you are on the path. How does your body feel? What images enter your mind? Observe the present moment with mindfulness.

This journal is meant to be used in any way that works for you. For example, you might like to tear out the pages before journaling on them and respond to the question on the back of the labyrinth image, or paste the page your daily journal, or display the labyrinth pages like a prayer flag.

See your time playing on the pages as breathing time for your soul – a time when no results are expected, a time when you are in the present moment, a time when you allow your soul to catch up with you.

May your hand and pen guide you towards inner peace and joy,
Catherine

through soles of feet into wide open sky this is turning
is is listening to bones of body
this is letting go of heaviness
prayer this is one slow
this is gratitude for joy
peace this is not walking this is
through soles of feet into wi
this is slowing down
this is not walking
this is not stepping inwards
growth this is moving closer to
ing the ground with reverence
deep within this is breathing
this is stepping messages from deep within

Entering the Labyrinth

This is not walking.
This is touching the ground with reverence.
This is stepping inwards.
This is slowing down.
This is listening to the bones of body,
receiving messages from deep within.
This is breathing through soles of feet
into wide open sky.
This is turning toward Self.

This is not walking.
This is awareness of senses.
This is letting go of heaviness.
This is one slow step at a time,
time slowing.
This is embodied prayer.
This is gratitude for joy, for sorrow,
for each opening to growth.
This is moving closer to Peace.

Catherine Anderson

ASK YOURSELF

Don't ask yourself what the world needs;
ask yourself what makes you come alive.
And then go and do that.
Because what the world needs is
people who have come alive.
Howard Thurman

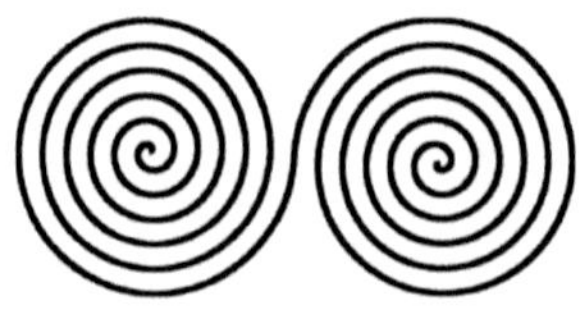

EXPLORE ON THE LABYRINTH PATH

What makes you come alive?

A NEW MORNING

This, I thought, is how great visionaries and
poets see everything - as if for the first time.
Each morning they see a new world
before their eyes; they do not really see it,
they create it.
Nikos Kazantzakis

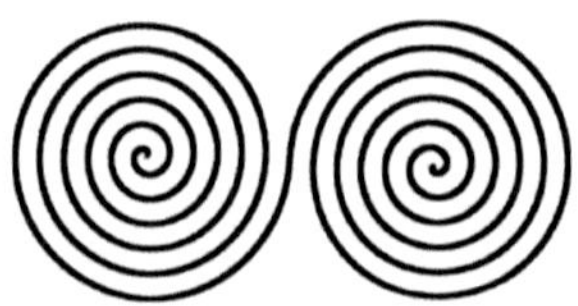

EXPLORE ON THE LABYRINTH PATH

How does it feel to be able to start today to create your new world?

MAKE SPACE

When you recover or discover something
that nourishes your soul and brings joy,
care enough about yourself
to make room for it in your life.
Jean Shinoda Bolen

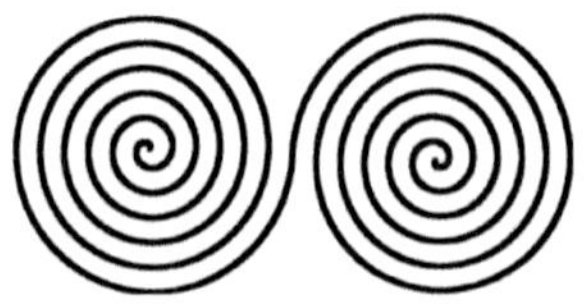

EXPLORE ON THE LABYRINTH PATH

*Where can you create space in your daily routine
for those things that nourish your soul
and bring you joy?*

TRUST YOUR JOY

Follow your bliss and don't be afraid,
and doors will open where
you didn't know they were going to be.
If you follow your bliss, doors will open for you
that wouldn't have opened for anyone else.
Joseph Campbell

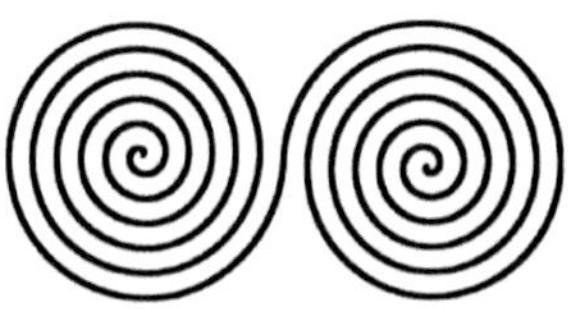

EXPLORE ON THE LABYRINTH PATH

What would you be doing today
if you were following your bliss?

JUST BEGIN

Whatever you can do,
or dream you can do, begin it.
Boldness has genius, power and magic in it.
Begin it now.
Johann Wolfgang von Goethe

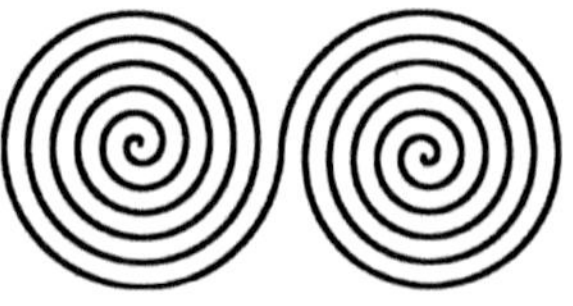

EXPLORE ON THE LABYRINTH PATH

*What dream can you begin
to bring to life today?*

CHOOSE ADVENTURE

Life is either
a daring adventure
or nothing.
Helen Keller

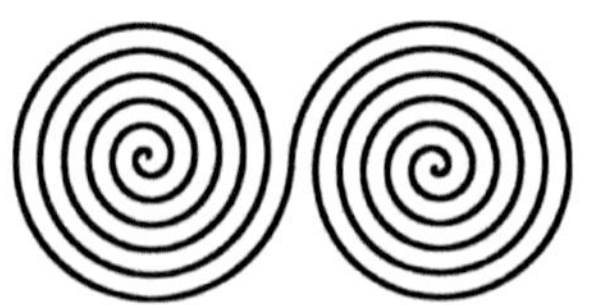

EXPLORE ON THE LABYRINTH PATH

*What would your life look like
if you lived it as a daring adventure?*

YOUR TRUE NORTH

If one advances confidently in the direction of his dreams, and endeavors to live the life which he has imagined, he will meet with a success unexpected in common hours.
Henry David Thoreau

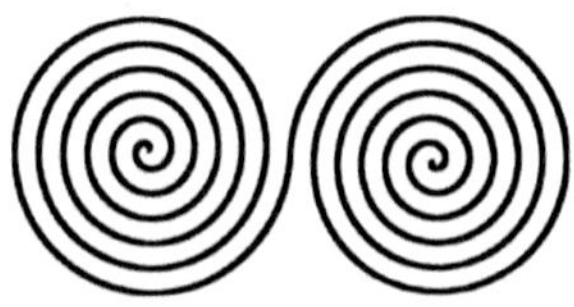

EXPLORE ON THE LABYRINTH PATH

What does success look like to you?

LIVING IN THE NOW

You don't get to choose how you're
going to die. Or when.
You can decide how you're going
to live now.
Joan Baez

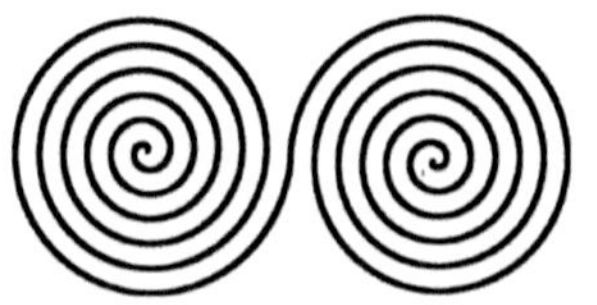

EXPLORE ON THE LABYRINTH PATH

If you believed you only had three more years to live, what would you choose to do during those years?

THE TIME IS RIGHT

I have now learned that there is never a wrong time to do something meaningful and courageous in life, something that makes you deeply and achingly happy. There is only a right time.
Wade Rouse

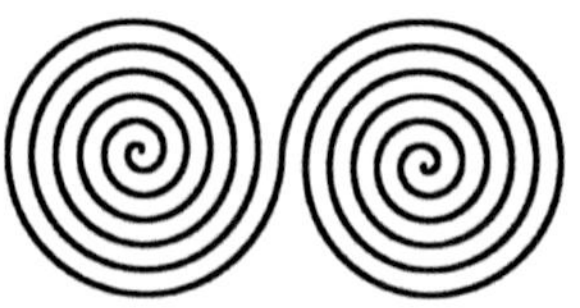

EXPLORE ON THE LABYRINTH PATH

What courageous and meaningful step can you take today?

FACING YOUR FEAR

If you have no anxiety, the risk you face
is probably not worthy of you.
Only risks you have outgrown
don't frighten you.
David Viscott

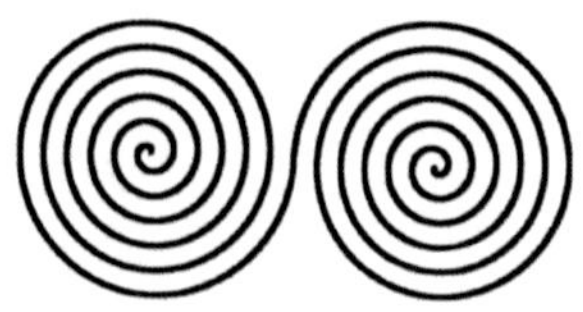

EXPLORE ON THE LABYRINTH PATH

*Unload your worries and anxiety
on the labyrinth path.*

FINDING YOUR COURAGE

You gain strength and courage and confidence
by every experience in which you really stop
to look fear in the face.
Eleanor Roosevelt

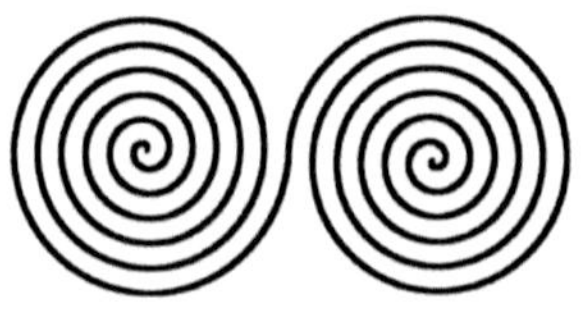

EXPLORE ON THE LABYRINTH PATH

Meet your fear on the labyrinth path
and ask it what it is trying to protect you from.
Let fear answer you.

YOU ARE UNIQUE

There is a vitality, a life force, an energy,
a quickening, that is translated through you
into action, and because there is only one of you
in all time, this expression is unique.
And if you block it, it will never exist through
any other medium and it will be lost.
Martha Graham

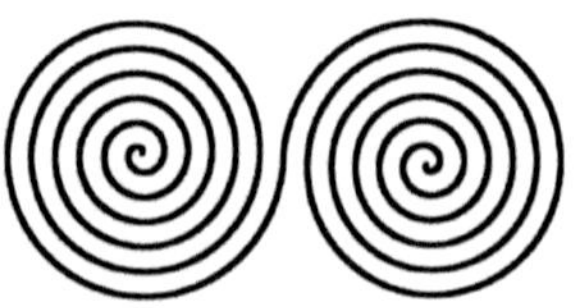

EXPLORE ON THE LABYRINTH PATH

How does it feel to have something unique to share with the world?

SAY NO

One way to come to say yes
is to say no to everything
that does not nourish and entice
our secret inner life out into the world.
David Whyte

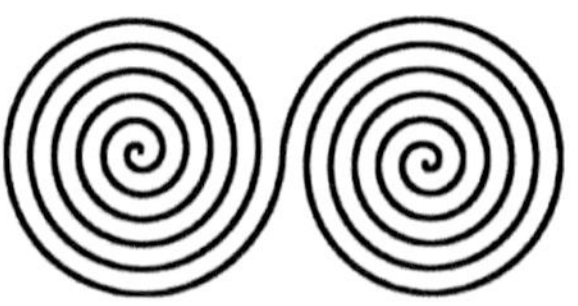

EXPLORE ON THE LABYRINTH PATH

Where do you need to say no,
so that you can answer the larger yes?

LIFE CHANGES

The minute you begin to do what you want to do,
it's really a different kind of life.
R. Buckminster Fuller

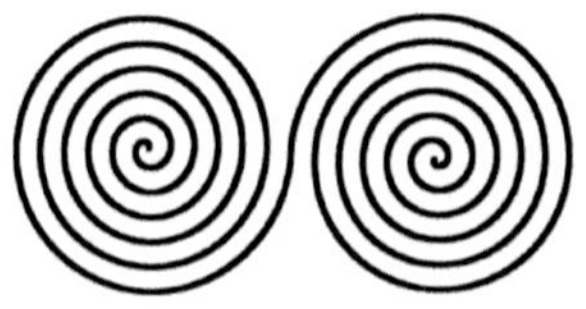

EXPLORE ON THE LABYRINTH PATH

How will your life be different
when you start following your heart?

EACH DAY COUNTS

What then shall I do this morning?
How we spend our days is, of course,
how we spend our lives.
What we do with this hour,
and that one, is what we are doing.
Annie Dillard

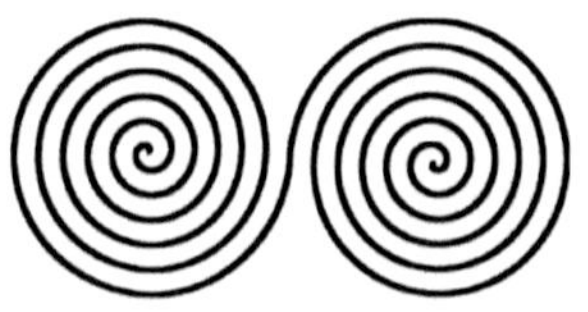

EXPLORE ON THE LABYRINTH PATH

What would your day look like if you were doing what you believe you are here to do?

CHOOSE JOY

If your spiritual and personal
journey doesn't have any fun in it,
then you ain't doing it right. Listen closer.
God wants you to live in joy.
Elizabeth Gilbert

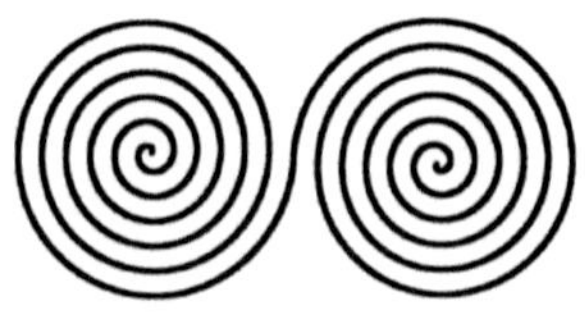

EXPLORE ON THE LABYRINTH PATH

What do you like to do for fun and laughter?

FOLLOW THE HEART PATH

Look at every path closely and deliberately,
then ask this crucial question:
Does this path have heart?
If it does, then the path is good.
If it doesn't, it is of no use.
Carlos Castaneda

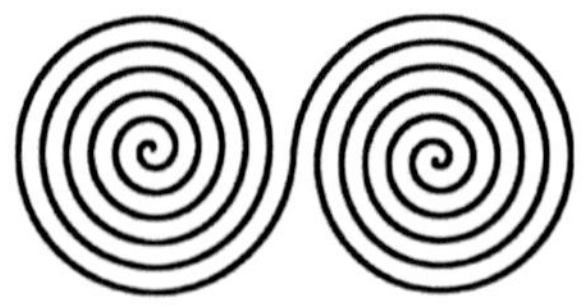

EXPLORE ON THE LABYRINTH PATH

How does your chosen path add light,
hope and joy to the world?

IT IS POSSIBLE

Start by doing what's necessary,
then what's possible -
and suddenly you are doing
the impossible.
St. Francis of Assisi

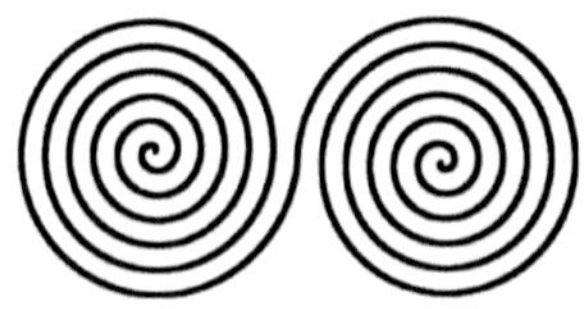

EXPLORE ON THE LABYRINTH PATH

Each step you take makes a difference.
What is it possible for you to do today?

EXPAND YOUR LIFE

Life shrinks and expands
in proportion to one's courage.
Anaïs Nin

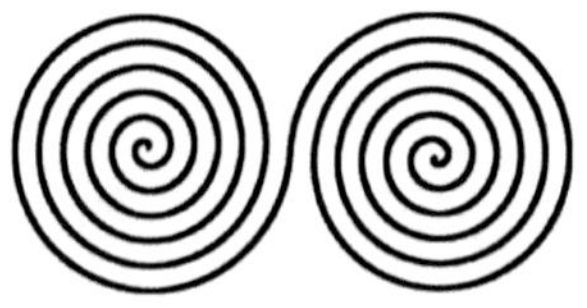

EXPLORE ON THE LABYRINTH PATH

What does an expanded life look like?

SEEK AND YOU WILL FIND

All things I seek are
now seeking me.
Florence Scovel Shinn

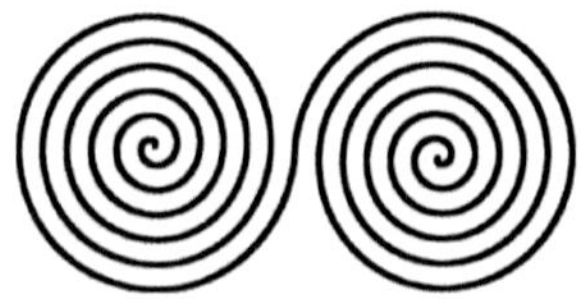

EXPLORE ON THE LABYRINTH PATH

Imagine that what you are looking for is also looking for you. Describe your meeting on the path.

CO-CREATION

It is our duty to proceed
as if limits to our ability do not exist.
We are collaborators in creation.
Teilhard de Chardin

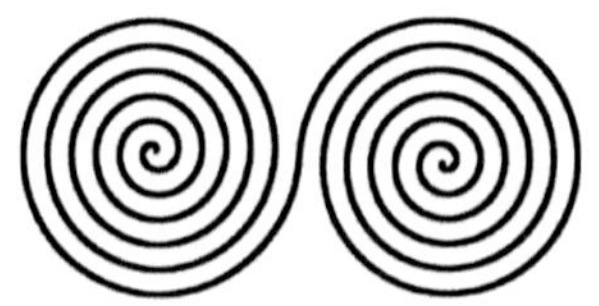

EXPLORE ON THE LABYRINTH PATH

*If you knew that you were collaborating
with creation by bringing your dream to life,
how would you proceed?*

THE GIFT OF TIME

Time, indeed, is a sacred gift,
and each day is a little life.
John Lubbock

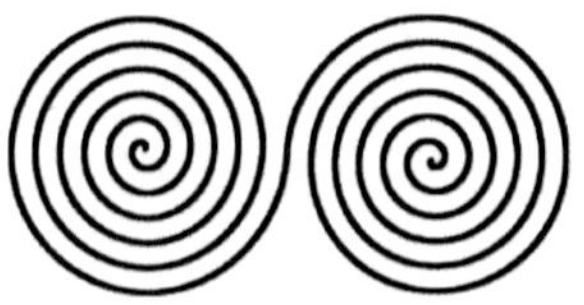

EXPLORE ON THE LABYRINTH PATH

How will you use this gift of time today?

ACT

Taking action always
breeds clarity.
Mike Dooley

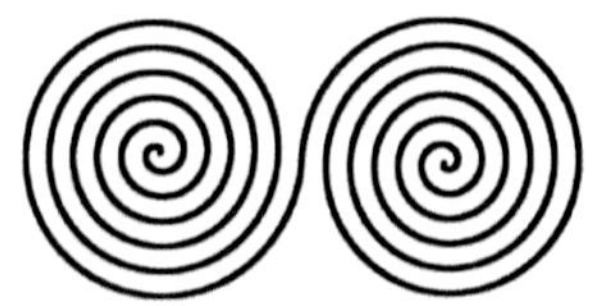

EXPLORE ON THE LABYRINTH PATH

Even wrong actions are valuable as they show us where we need to take a U-turn. What is the next action you can take and what clarity does it bring?

SLOW AND STEADY

Be not afraid of growing slowly.
Be afraid of standing still.
Chinese Proverb

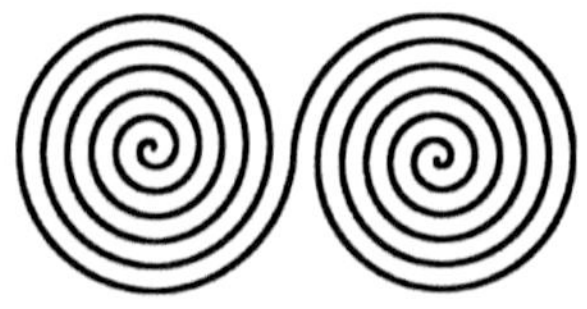

EXPLORE ON THE LABYRINTH PATH

*We often judge ourselves for not being enough.
List all the steps you have made in the right direction,
even the steps taken along the scenic path.*

OPENING SPACE

Take an action every day that alleviates suffering
or completes something old, so you can
make more space for the new.
Angeles Arrien

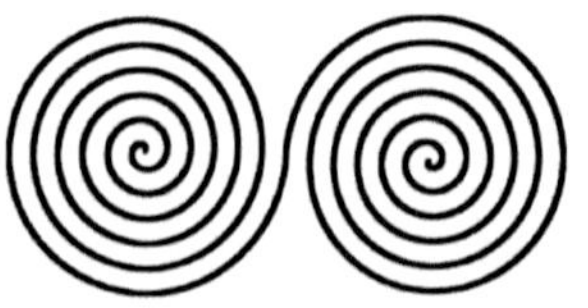

EXPLORE ON THE LABYRINTH PATH

*What can you let go of or clear out today
to make space for new opportunities to enter your life?*

YOU ARE DESERVING

We cannot achieve more in life
than what we believe in our heart of hearts
we deserve to have.
James R. Ball

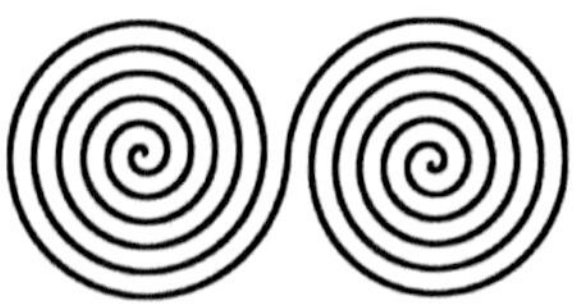

EXPLORE ON THE LABYRINTH PATH

*List all the reasons you deserve
to live a life you love.*

THE INGREDIENTS

Risk-taking, trust and serendipity
are key ingredients of joy.
Without risk, nothing new ever happens.
Without trust, fear creeps in.
Without serendipity, there are no surprises.
Rita Golden Gelman

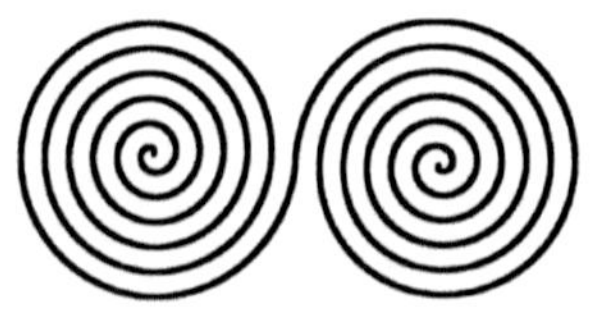

EXPLORE ON THE LABYRINTH PATH

*Where on your path have synchronicity
and serendipity surprised and delighted you?*

RE-ENCHANTMENT

It is up to us to re-enchant this planet earth.
Up to us to midwife at our own rebirth.
Will Ashe Bacon

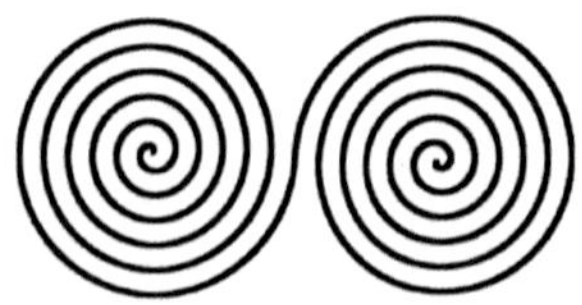

EXPLORE ON THE LABYRINTH PATH

How can you support and encourage yourself as you give birth to your dream?

YOUR DESTINY

It is better to live your own destiny imperfectly
than to live an imitation of somebody else's life
with perfection.
Bhagavad Gita

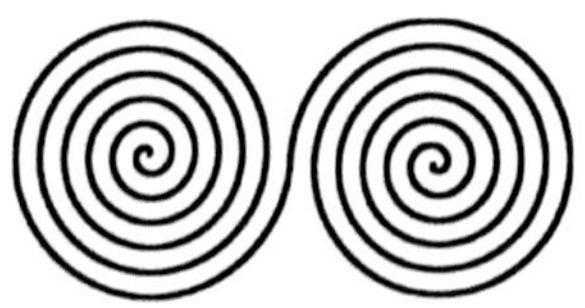

EXPLORE ON THE LABYRINTH PATH

*Your destiny may take you along an untrodden path.
What do you need to take along on this journey to support you
as you walk through uncharted territory?*

BE YOURSELF

The privilege of a lifetime
is being who you are.
Joseph Campbell

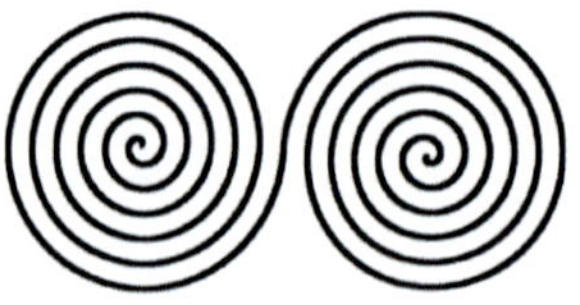

EXPLORE ON THE LABYRINTH PATH

Who are you? Begin with the words
"I am one who ..."

ASK YOURSELF

Don't ask yourself what the world needs;
ask yourself what makes you come alive.
And then go and do that.
Because what the world needs is
people who have come alive.
Howard Thurman

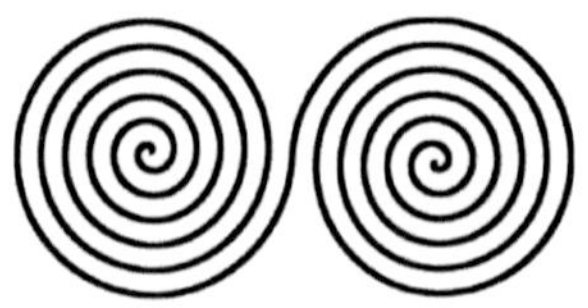

EXPLORE ON THE LABYRINTH PATH

What makes you come alive?

About Catherine

Catherine has two labyrinths in her backyard – an eleven circuit medieval design and a seven circuit classical design – which she walks as a way to center, slow down and listen for messages from her soul. Her love of the labyrinth led her to train with Rev. Dr. Lauren Artress to become a certified Veriditas Labyrinth Facilitator in 2009 and an Advanced Labyrinth Facilitator Training in 2013. She is now on the faculty of Veriditas.

Meeting Your Soul on the Labyrinth: SoulCollage® and the Labyrinth as Pathways for Transformation is Catherine's most recent book. It focuses on using the SoulCollage® process created by Seena Frost with walking the labyrinth to deepen and integrate your personal experience. As a SoulCollage® Facilitator and SoulCollage® Trainer, Catherine loves showing others how to use this transformational collage process.

Catherine is also author of *The Creative Photographer* and loves teaching photography as mindfulness practice in beautiful places around the world. She has published a number of imagery books that can be used without restriction in personal art (such as SoulCollage®, art journals, collage art and crafts) which include *Portals, Pathways and Labyrinths,* a resource for labyrinth images.

For more information, or to order books for groups at group pricing, visit Catherine's website

www.creativepilgrimage.com

Made in United States
North Haven, CT
03 November 2025